Happy Birthday Brother!

YOU ARE THE BIRTHDAY BOY!

LET'S CELEBRATE, BROTHER!

YOU ARE SO AMAZING!

BROTHER, IT'S PARTY TIME!

TODAY IS THE DAY TO BE HAPPY!

BROTHER, BIRTHDAY CHEERS!

THIS IS YOUR SPECIAL DAY!

BROTHER, IT'S TIME TO MAKE A BIRTHDAY WISH!

BELIEVE IN MAGIC!

HIP! HIP! HOORAY! BROTHER!

YOU ARE AWESOME!

HAPPY
BIRTHDAY

HAPPY BIRTHDAY BROTHER! COLORING CARD

www.ingramcontent.com/pod-product-compliance
Lightning Source LLC
Chambersburg PA
CBHW070024260726
48658CB00003B/1032